Anne-Dorthe Grigaff

Knitted Animals

photographs: Bjarni B. Jacobsen

Hawthorn Press

First published in Denmark in 2005 by Forlaget Olivia,
under the title *Strikkede dyr* © Olivia, Copenhagen 2005

Anne-Dorthe Grigaff is hereby identified as author of this work in accordance with Section 77
of the Copyright, Designs and Patent Act, 1988. She asserts and gives notice of her moral right
under this Act.

Published by Hawthorn Press, Hawthorn House, 1 Lansdown Lane, Stroud, Gloucestershire,
GL5 1BJ, UK Tel: (01453) 757040 Fax: (01453) 751138 E-mail: info@hawthornpress.com
www.hawthornpress.com

With thanks to Solspejlet, Frederiksborggade 41, 1360 Copenhagen K., Denmark, for kindly
lending the wooden toys photographed in this book

English edition *Knitted Animals* © Hawthorn Press 2006
Translated by Irena Tully, www.impulsefilms.com
Photographs by Bjarni B. Jacobsen
Book design by Anne-Dorthe Grigaff
Typesetting in English version by Hawthorn Press, Stroud, Gloucestershire
Printed by Kristianstad Book Printers Ltd, Sweden

Mixed Sources
Product group from well-managed
forests and other controlled sources
www.fsc.org Cert. no. SGS-COC-2086
© 1996 Forest Stewardship Council
FSC

British Library Cataloguing in Publication Data applied for

ISBN-10 1 903458 68 4   ISBN-13 978-1 903458-68-6

Contents

Foreword

Making toys for children is in itself a pleasurable pastime for adults, as we can nourish parts of ourselves that we otherwise too often ignore in our busy everyday lives. This activity gives us an opportunity to withdraw and be at peace with our thoughts for a while, allowing space for a creative process.

In knitted animals made by parents or grandparents, both love and joy are woven together like invisible material. Consequently this gift, this special toy, will be received differently from one that can be replaced just by returning to the shop.

Of course, a small cat or other knitted animal can come apart or be misplaced, but there is something especially comforting about getting a 'little sister cat' for the one that has been lost. Maybe the child has been fortunate enough to see how the toy was made. The amazement at what adults can create with their skilled hands will make the pleasure all the greater and the grief easier to bear.

Many of the models are so easy to knit that older children, too, can make them – especially with some grown-up help to hand.

At school one day I met a father who told me that his 10-year-old son was a keen knitter and very much enjoyed knitting when he got up in the mornings. He did not watch children's TV programmes like other children, and the father admitted that he found it a bit strange to see his son sitting there knitting. It struck me that this child had probably found a reflective, peaceful space, and a creative activity he enjoyed. We talked a little more about why it is good for children to knit. Afterwards the father saw how knitting could benefit the boy, and was more understanding – even proud.

A good time for children to learn to knit is around seven years of age, when their motor skills can cope with the challenge. The child learns by imitating the adult. At the school where I work, the 14 to 15-year-old pupils are invited to team up with pupils aged 7-8 years. The older pupils sit the younger ones on their lap and show them how to knit. In this way younger pupils quickly learn how to knit and at the same time form a social bond with the older ones, who are flattered by the confidence the younger children show in their abilities.

In learning to knit the child also practises coordination, fine-tunes motor skills and uses logical thinking. Modern brain researchers and neurobiologists confirm that practical abilities and cognitive skills are learned through the body: grasping things with the hands forms the basis for later grasping things with the mind too. But

quite apart from technical abilities, learning to knit also develops a child's sense of aesthetics and beauty.

The wonderful thing about teaching children to knit at an early age is that their senses are so open and they find it so natural to learn through the body. They are still at the stage where they want to do the things they see adults doing. They gain great pleasure from making things that are handy and useful, especially as small gifts for the family. It is important to find activities appropriate for the age of the child, and small objects that are fun to play with, like those in this book. Several of them are little more than a square that forms the basis for a small animal. Initially the adult can sew the animal together, although very soon the child will want to do it on his or

her own. By all means let the child do so, and help only when it is absolutely necessary. Children will be very proud when they see what a simple little square can be made into. There is added mystery in the flat shape transforming into a rounded shape. Of course, you do not need to explain all this to children; just let them experience it and thrill to life's mysteries. Later on the experience can be recalled in geometry.

An old Chinese proverb says: 'Show me and I see, tell me and I remember, involve me and I understand.'

Consider, also, that knitting brings the child into close contact with the yarn and the knitting needles. Give the child the best, preferably natural materials. This provides a good sensory experience and teaches the child, for instance, about the warmth-giving qualities of wool or the cooling qualities of flax and cotton. I think it is best to start with wool, however, because it is more flexible and easier for the child to work with. It smells wonderful and if you opt for wooden knitting needles the child gets a good, versatile needle that offers less resistance than metal needles.

At the school where I work we recite the following verse before we start teaching the smaller pupils:

'Train your hands

Make busy your arms

Practice the clear power of thought

With the warm-heartedness of art

In your hand sleeps the spirit'

Much wisdom lies hidden in this verse. As an adult I often marvel at it, because it formulates succinctly what would otherwise take many words to explain.

Have fun knitting with your child!

Anne-Dorthe Grigaff

Materials & technique

See also the Glossary for
needle sizes and explanation of stitches.

Yarns

The materials are as natural as can be. When children encounter natural materials, their sensory experience is enhanced. As a rule I mix two different types of yarn in order to achieve the best possible colour and surface structure. This gives a living surface that is much more animal-like. Often wool is mixed with silk, or a bouclé yarn with a smooth yarn. Knitting is also a touch faster with two yarns, making it easier to form the animal. Once you have discovered this method, the possibilities are endless and enable completely new means of expression using just one type of yarn. Leftover yarns gain a new lease of life, and even the yarns from old, discarded sweaters can be reused for their structural quality. Aim to use yarns or combinations of yarns that reflect the colours and characteristics of each animal, and select the needle size accordingly.

All these patterns can also be knitted using single yarns, which may be more suitable for new and inexperienced knitters. If you knit with a single yarn, the yarn packaging will indicate the appropriate size. As a rough guide, use 3 to 3.25mm with 4 ply, 4mm with double knit or doubled 4 ply and 4.5 to 5mm with chunky or doubled double knit. Choice of yarn and needle size can also be exploited to vary the scale of the animals.

Stuffing

The animals can be stuffed with wool, but for people who are allergic to wool it may be necessary to use another material e.g. web of carded cotton fibres, kapok or something similar. You should also keep allergy issues in mind when choosing yarns.

Knitting needles

I use wooden needles which enhance the pleasure of knitting, and have more advantages than metal and bamboo needles. They become smoother with time, more beautiful, and using them is beneficial if one is prone to sore joints, since they are more 'springy'. Why not turn knitting into something thoroughly enjoyable?

Mother duck with small ducklings

Materials

Duck-coloured yarn. A double-knit mohair and white alpaca can be used, which makes the duck really soft.
Needle size: as appropriate for yarn used
Carded wool for stuffing

The eyes are sewn on in a black or dark colour. In this case dark blue is used. The beak is sewn using left-over orange woollen yarn. See drawings on page 14.

Mother duck

BODY: cast on 30 stitches and work 20 rows in garter stitch. Cast off loosely.
HEAD: cast on 16 stitches and work 12 rows in garter stitch. Cast off.

Ducklings

BODY: cast on 15 stitches and work 10 rows in garter stitch. Cast off.
HEAD: cast on 8 stitches and work 6 rows in garter stitch. Cast off.

To make up:

BODY: fold the body lengthwise and sew it together at the top and sides. Make sure that the body rounds out nicely at the corners. Make the tail end pointed when sewing it together. Stuff with wool so the body becomes firm and oval-shaped with a pointed tail. Sew bottom edge.

HEAD: fold the head and sew it together. Make it as round as possible. Stuff it with wool and sew it onto the body.

BEAK: make the beak out of left-over orange woollen yarn. Sew it in overlapping buttonhole stitch so a round duck-like beak emerges.

EYES: sew in dark yarn, approximately 2-3 stitches.

1.

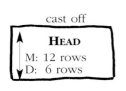

cast off

HEAD
M: 12 rows
D: 6 rows

MOTHER cast on
16 stitches
DUCKLING: cast on
8 stitches

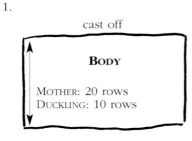

cast off

BODY

MOTHER: 20 rows
DUCKLING: 10 rows

MOTHER cast on 30 stitches
DUCKLING: cast on 15 stitches

HEAD 3.

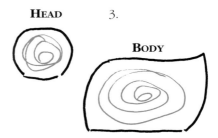

BODY

fill with wool and sew at the bottom

2.

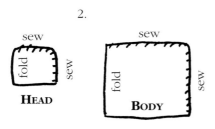

sew

fold   sew

HEAD

sew

fold   sew

BODY

4.

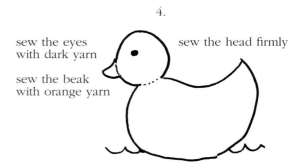

sew the eyes
with dark yarn

sew the head firmly

sew the beak
with orange yarn

Sweet, soft little ducklings that quack after Mother and find their place in line. It's nice feeding the ducks and watching them rush after the bread that you help break into small pieces. Lovely toys for young park visitors.

Growly bear with big heavy paws

Materials

Hairy effect yarn
Tweed yarn
Needle size: 3.5mm
Carded wool for stuffing

The yarn I have used here is very hairy effect yarn of wool and mohair mixed with a tweed yarn to give good close knitting. The bear is knitted on 3.5mm needles to achieve the tightest knitting possible. The long 'bear fur' must be fished out with a knitting needle or needle, so that as much fur as possible is on the outside. Start at the back and knit towards the nose. Then continue knitting to make the bear's under-side. The bear is knitted all in one piece (stocking stitch) except for the ears (garter stitch). See drawing on page 19.

BODY: cast on 16 stitches. Starting with a purl row work in stocking stitch. Increase 1 stitch at either end of the 2nd row. Work the 3rd row with no shaping (purl). Cast on 10 stitches at the beginning of the 4th and 5th rows. Now you have begun to knit the back legs.

Increase 2 stitches at the centre of the 6th row to form the bear's spinal column. It should bend upwards a little where the hip is. At this point you should have 40 stitches on your needle. Work 4 rows. Finish the shaping for the back legs by casting off 10 stitches at the beginning of the 10th and 11th rows. Decrease 2 stitches in the centre of the 12th row (18 stitches remain) so that the spinal column now bends downwards. Work 4 rows for the tummy. Cast on 10 stitches at the beginning of the 16th and 17th rows, and increase by 2 stitches at the centre of the 18th row for the bear's shoulders.

Cast off 12 stitches at the beginning of the 22nd and 23rd rows for the neck, and decrease by 2 stitches at the centre of the work. At this point you should have 16 stitches on your needle.

NECK AND HEAD: work 1-2 rows. The last row should be a purl row. Work the next

row as follows: knit 1 stitch, knit 2 together, knit 3, knit 2 together, knit 3, knit 2 together, knit 1.

Work 2 rows without shaping. On the following row decrease 1 stitch at the beginning and end of the row (11 stitches). Work 2 rows. On the following knit row: knit 1 stitch, increase 1 stitch, knit 2, increase 1 stitch, knit 2, increase 1 stitch, knit 1. Purl 1 row.

Next knit row: knit 3, increase 1 stitch, knit 4, increase 1 stitch, knit 3.

Work 2 rows.

The purl row: purl 3, decrease 1 stitch, purl 4, decrease 1 stitch, purl 3.

Work 2 rows.

The knit row: knit 2, decrease 1 stitch, knit 2, decrease 1 stitch, knit 2.

Work 2 rows.

The purl row: purl 2, knit 2 stitches together, 4 times altogether, purl 2.

Work 2 rows.

The knit row: knit 1, decrease 1 stitch, knit 2, decrease 1 stitch.

Purl 1 row.

Knit 2 stitches together 3 times.

Now you are starting to knit the bear's underside: work 3 rows. On the following row: increase 1 stitch at the beginning and end of the row. Work 8 rows.

Once again, increase 1 stitch at the beginning and end of the following row. Work 9 rows.

Repeat on the following row, increasing at the beginning and end of the row.

Now for the tummy part of the body: cast on 6 stitches at either end of the next row. Work 6 rows. Cast off 8 stitches at the beginning and end of the next row for each leg and work 6 rows (tummy).

Cast on 8 stitches at either end of the next row for the back legs. Work 6 rows.

For rows 2 and 3, decrease 1 stitch at the centre of the work. Cast off.

EARS: cast on 5 stitches and work 3 rows in garter stitch. Cast off 1 stitch at the beginning of the next 2 rows. Cast off the last 3 stitches. Work the other ear exactly the same.

To make up:

Sew the underside to the upper body. The underside is somewhat smaller, so you may need to stretch it to fit. Leave the rear open so that you can stuff the bear with wool until it is firm and begins to take shape. Stuffing the bear may be a bit difficult and you will probably need to shape it a little after it has been stuffed, but you should be able to manage, using a needle and thread. Add a few stitches in the body and head, or wherever you think the bear needs a bit more shape, until you are satisfied.

It is a good idea to go to the zoo and study bears thoroughly, or borrow some books from the library that contain good colour pictures of bears. This can really help.

Otherwise you can easily make a strange animal such as a 'crocofant' or some such thing if you do not have the bear's natural form before you.

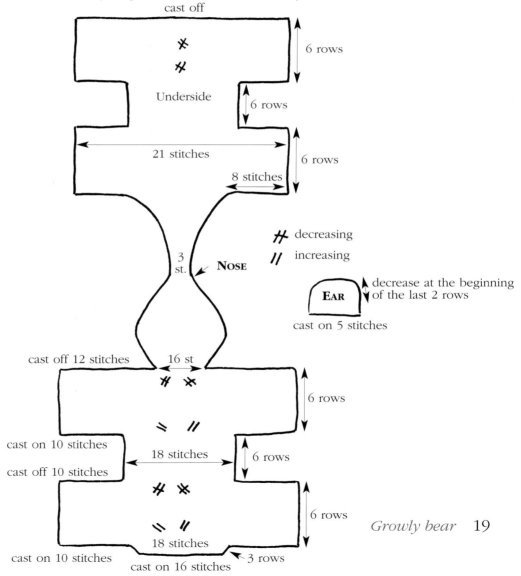

cast off

Underside

6 rows

6 rows

21 stitches

6 rows

8 stitches

decreasing

increasing

3 st.

NOSE

EAR

decrease at the beginning of the last 2 rows

cast on 5 stitches

cast off 12 stitches

16 st

6 rows

cast on 10 stitches

18 stitches

6 rows

cast off 10 stitches

18 stitches

6 rows

cast on 10 stitches

3 rows

cast on 16 stitches

Growly bear 19

It is safe and warm here in the
soft sheep's wool or lamb's wool.
Ready to cuddle up with.

Soft sheep & lamb

Materials

Mohair-bouclé or other wool bouclé
Needle size: to suit yarn used
Carded wool for stuffing
Crochet needle

There are three possible sizes, with the middle size shown in brackets.

BODY: cast on 36 (24) 18 stitches and work in garter stitch until you have 10 (8) 6 rows. Cast off 8 (6) 4 stitches at the beginning and end of the next row, breaking and rejoining the yarn as necessary. Work a further 10 (8) 6 rows. Cast on 8 (6) 4 stitches at either end of the next row. Work 10 (8) 6 rows and decrease by casting off 12 (8) 4 stitches at either end of the next row. Work 24 (16) 12 rows. Cast off.

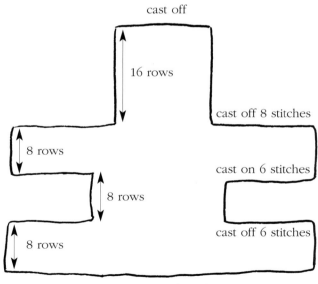

cast off

16 rows

cast off 8 stitches

8 rows

cast on 6 stitches

8 rows

cast off 6 stitches

8 rows

cast on e.g. 24 stitches

To make up:

Sew the legs and tummy together. Leave the rear of the sheep open for stuffing.

Roll the wool into a firm 'sausage' and press it down into the leg. Do the same with the other legs.

You can roll the wool tightly around a knitting needle, or narrow pointed scissors, and press it down into the leg. Press the knitting needle/scissors with your right hand, while holding the leg with your left hand. While the right hand is stuffing, the left hand is shaping. Don't stuff the head and tummy too hard.

Sew the rear of the sheep together.

Crochet the tail as a row of chain stitches. Shape the ears using a short row of chain stitches and sew them to each side of the head with several stitches.

Crochet some wool on with a couple of stitches.

Sew the legs into a long 'tube' and sew them together at the head and tail. Fill the tummy with wool and sew it together.

Teddy bear

Materials

Approx. 100g mohair bouclé
Needle size: 3.5mm and a long doll's needle
Carded wool for stuffing
A small piece of leather
Black pearl yarn for the nose (pearl yarn is mercerised cotton, which is slightly glossy)

BODY AND HEAD: begin with the head. Cast on 35 stitches. Work in stocking stitch to a length of 9cm. Decrease 10 stitches evenly spaced along the next row. Continue until the body measures 20cm, finishing with a purl row. Decrease 5 stitches evenly spaced over the next row.
Work 3 rows. Decrease 5 stitches on the next row as before. Purl 1 row. Decrease 5 stitches on the next row. Purl 1 row. Decrease 5 stitches in the next row. Cast off.

ARMS: cast on 14 stitches. Work in stocking stitch until the work measures approx. 11cm, finishing with a purl row. Decrease on the next row as follows: knit 2 stitches together, knit 1, knit 2 stitches together. Purl 1 row. Decrease again on the next row as before. Cast off.

LEGS: cast on 14 stitches. Work in stocking stitch until the work measures 8cm, finishing with a purl row. Cast on 3 stitches at the start of the next 2 rows. Purl 1 row. Increase 1 stitch at each end of the next row. Work 4 rows. Decrease 1 stitch at each end of the purl row. Cast off knitwise.

NOSE: cast on 14 stitches. Work in stocking stitch to produce a square. Cast off.

To make up:

BODY AND HEAD: sew up the seam of the body and the head. Avoid sewing all the way down, as there has to be an opening for the wool stuffing. Turn inside out. The bear looks nicest with the wrong side out as it is not as 'stripy' as the plain side.
Roll a firm ball of wool into the head part, about the size of a tennis ball. Tighten well around the ball and make sure that it is a nice, harmonious round shape. Mould the wool a little, as it does not matter if there is

a small 'tail' on the ball. You can push it down into the neck part. Tie around the neck with a double thread (the same thread).

Fill the body with the wool and sew it together. Shape the body until it is oblong, well-proportioned and firm. More wool may be needed than you might initially imagine, and it requires some ingenuity and practice to stuff the bear. If it is not tightly stuffed, it quickly becomes too floppy.

Sew together at the bottom and fasten the yarn by sewing it in and out of the bear. The wool stuffing helps to prevent the fastening coming undone. Pull the ears forward a little and sew them into shape without stuffing with wool.

NOSE: sew the nose on like a 'clown nose' – a little bit loosely so it is baggy. Leave the last side open for stuffing.

Roll another firm ball and stuff it in. Sew the last side firmly.

Shape the nose a little so it looks cute.

LEGS AND ARMS: sew the legs and arms together so that they are open at the top. Fill with wool little by little, again very firmly. Both legs should be the same thickness and the feet the same size with the same amount of stuffing.

Sew the arms together and stuff them in the same way. Sew up the top.

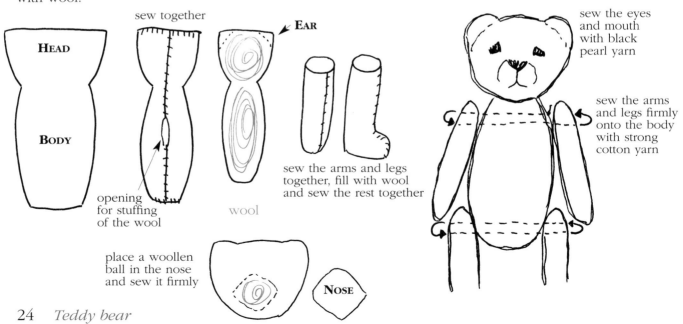

sew together

HEAD

BODY

opening for stuffing of the wool

place a woollen ball in the nose and sew it firmly

← **EAR**

wool

sew the arms and legs together, fill with wool and sew the rest together

NOSE

sew the eyes and mouth with black pearl yarn

sew the arms and legs firmly onto the body with strong cotton yarn

SEW THE LEGS AND ARMS TO THE BODY: (see drawing) you will need a 'good eye' so the arms don't look as if they are growing out of the neck. They must be at shoulder height. Stick the long needle through the body and hang the legs or arms on it. Find a good position and don't sew the seams until you are satisfied.

Sew from the inside of the legs/arms through the body towards the other leg/arm. Tighten the thread. Sew the other way back and tighten afterwards so the arms/legs are joined firmly and tightly to the body. Sew a couple of times back and forth. Then the legs and arms can move up and down.

NOSE AND MOUTH: cut the leather into the shape of a nose and glue it on with textile glue. Hold the nose until the glue is dry. Sew around the leather with pearl yarn until it's completely covered. Sew on the mouth.

EYES: place the eyes right over the snout. It's a matter of taste how close the eyes should be to each other. Use a couple of pins of the same colour to mark where the eyes should be. They must sit right beside each other and must be sewn many times back and forth through the eyes in order to be visible. They can be round or square according to taste.

Now the teddy is ready for a hug.

Children love animals that are soft, and most children are familiar with cats. Getting a silky-soft cat which you have made is the nicest gift imaginable for a child.

Soft cuddly cats

Materials

Alpaca wool
Mohair yarn
2 balls of angora or other hairy yarn (one can also use home-woven yarn which can be brushed up afterwards)
Needle size: to suit yarn used
Carded wool for stuffing
A bit of pearl yarn for the eyes and the nose (if the cat is light coloured, blue eyes and a pink nose are nice. Otherwise black pearl yarn is best)

The size depends on how thick the yarn is and on the size of the needle. You can reduce the number of stitches according to the size you want. Just follow these rules:
* ★ the body is always square
* ★ the head is 2 squares long
* ★ the tail is 2/3 of the body length

BODY: start e.g. with 24 stitches: work in stocking stitch to form a square.
Cast off.

HEAD: cast on 12 stitches. Work in stocking stitch until you have a square. Measure and work the same number of rows again so it is twice as long. Cast off.
TAIL: cast on 6 stitches and work 2/3 of the body length. Cast off.

To make up:

Fold the corners of the body towards each other so you have four little cornets (see drawing). Join the seams with overcast stitch until there is a little open hole in the middle. Fill it with wool, form the body and sew it together under the tummy. The wool must be pressed well into the paws.

Fold the head in the middle so a little 'bag' is created. Roll a woollen ball for stuffing the head, and roll another little ball and put

it in like a nose. Gather the head into the neck and sew it firmly onto the body. Pull the knitted head up a little where the ears will be. Sew them into shape. Sew up the tail. Stuff it with a little bit of wool and sew it firmly onto the body so it bends straight up. Put a bow around the neck with a little bell. Older children will love that. Young children can choke on bells, so it is not suitable for children under 3.

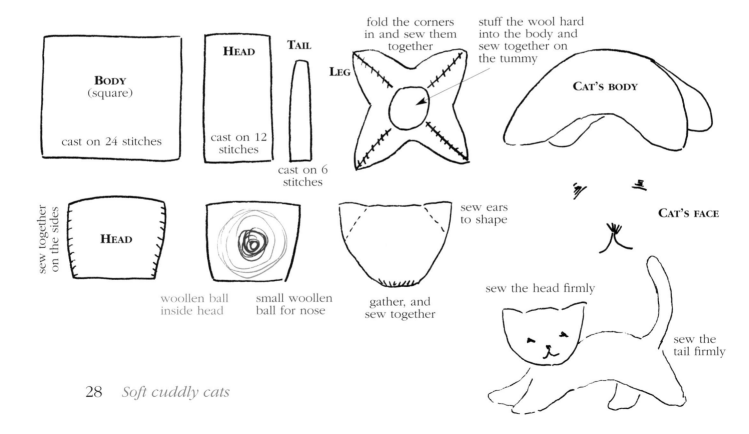

BODY (square)

cast on 24 stitches

HEAD

cast on 12 stitches

TAIL

cast on 6 stitches

LEG

fold the corners in and sew them together

stuff the wool hard into the body and sew together on the tummy

CAT'S BODY

sew together on the sides

HEAD

woollen ball inside head

small woollen ball for nose

gather, and sew together

sew ears to shape

CAT'S FACE

sew the head firmly

sew the tail firmly

Cuddly cheeky dogs

Materials

Mohair bouclé in a good doggy colour
Mohair yarn
Needle size: 4.5mm
Carded wool for stuffing
A bit of pearl yarn for the nose, mouth and eyes

BODY: cast on 26 stitches. Work 10 rows of stocking stitch. Cast off 6 stitches for each leg at the beginning and end of the next row, breaking and rejoining the yarn as necessary. Work 6 rows of stocking stitch on the remaining 14 stitches and then cast on another 6 stitches at either end of the next row for the legs. Work 10 rows of stocking stitch and cast off.

HEAD: cast on 14 stitches. Work 2 rows of stocking stitch. Increase 1 stitch at the beginning and end of each knit row, 3 times altogether. Finish with a purl row. Work 4 rows of stocking stitch and cast off.

EARS: cast on 5 stitches and work 3 rows. Start with a purl row. On the 4th row, knit the first and last 2 stitches together. Purl 1 row and cast off. Repeat with the other ear.

TAIL: cast on 6 stitches and work 15 rows of stocking stitch. Cast off 2 stitches at the beginning of the 16th and 17th rows. Purl the next row. Cast off.

They can be cheeky, they can be cuddly, they can get up to naughty tricks, and yet they are always a loyal friend and know exactly how you feel.

To make up:

Sew the legs together. Sew the dog's front and rear parts together with a 'gathering' thread. Leave an opening in the middle for the wool stuffing. Roll some wool tightly like a 'sausage' around pointed scissors and push it down into the leg. Hold the wool while you're pulling the scissors out. Repeat with the other leg. Roll a thick woollen 'sausage' for the body and push it in. Sew the dog together under the tummy.

Sew the head together, start at the top of the head and progress towards the nose and then from the nose towards the neck. Stuff with wool until the head is firm, and sew it onto the body. Sew the ears on and fold them in the desired position. You can sew the nose and eyes in position by sewing into the wool and tightening the thread a little. Sew the tail together and stuff it just like the legs. Sew it firmly to the rear of the body.

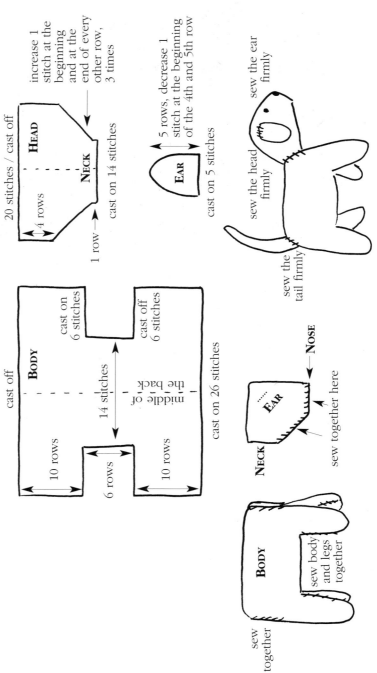

HEAD

20 stitches / cast off

increase 1 stitch at the beginning and at the end of every other row, 3 times

NECK

4 rows

1 row

cast on 14 stitches

EAR

5 rows, decrease 1 stitch at the beginning of the 4th and 5th row

cast on 5 stitches

sew the ear firmly

sew the head firmly

sew the head firmly

sew the tail firmly

BODY

cast off

cast on 6 stitches

cast off 6 stitches

14 stitches

middle of the back

10 rows

6 rows

10 rows

cast on 26 stitches

NECK

EAR

NOSE

sew together here

BODY

sew body and legs together

sew together

Squirrel

Materials

Mohair yarn, a thin woollen yarn, silk tweed. Together these three yarns give a good structure. Silk tweed gives good nuanced and frizzy knitting, and the mohair provides volume. The thin woollen yarn adds volume.

Needle size: 3mm

Carded wool for stuffing

BODY: cast on 20 stitches. Work 42 rows of stocking stitch. Cast off loosely.

HEAD: cast on 14 stitches. Work 8 rows. Cast off.

EARS: cast on 5 stitches. Work 2 rows. Decrease 1 stitch at the beginning of each row until 1 stitch remains. Break the yarn and pull it through the last stitch.

EAR
cast on 5 stitches
2 rows
decrease 1 stitch at the beginning of each row

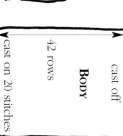

HEAD
8 rows
cast off
cast on 16 stitches

BODY
42 rows
cast off
cast on 20 stitches

To make up:

BODY: sew the body together in the same way as the cat on page 28, but the squirrel's back legs must be bigger than the front legs. Sew a little between the legs so they point the right way.

HEAD: fold the knitted piece and sew it together at the top and along one side. Gather it a little at the top so it is as round as possible – but the pointed part at the highest corner of the side must be pointed. That will be the nose. Stuff with wool until it feels nice and firm. Gather at the neck and sew the head firmly onto the body. It is absolutely necessary to shape the squirrel's head some more before you sew on the eyes and nose. Place the ears high and close together on the head.

TAIL: make this in the same way as the fox tail on page 48. The tail must be approximately as long as the squirrel's body and there must be space for it to bend a little. Sew it firmly and shape it so it has the right squirrel look.

Goosy Lucy from a storybook...

or the wild geese Danish children sing about.

Materials

Goose-coloured yarn (a combination of a natural coloured Shetland wool and a white and beige silk bouclé could be used.
Needle size: to suit yarn used
Carded wool for stuffing
Black wool yarn for the eyes, yellow/orange woollen yarn for the beak and the feet

UPPER BODY: cast on 4 stitches and work 2 rows garter stitch. Begin increasing for the body – increase 1 stitch at the beginning and end of the next row. Work 1 row and repeat, increasing on every other row until there are 24 stitches (21 rows).
Work 12 rows. Begin decreasing for the neck by knitting 2 stitches together at the beginning and end of every other row until there are 10 stitches left.
Work a further 12 rows on the neck until there are 58 rows in total. Increase 3 stitches on the next row, 1 at either end and 1 in the centre. Work another 6 rows and cast off.
BREAST PART: cast on 2 stitches. Work 3 rows. (Increase at the beginning and end of the next row, and knit 4 rows) twice. (Increase at the beginning and end of the next row, and knit 3 rows) twice. Increase at the beginning and end of the next row (12 stitches altogether). Continue without shaping until there are 36 rows. Begin decreasing at the beginning and end of every other row until there are 2 stitches left. Cast off.
FEET: cast on 2 stitches. Knit 1 row. Increase 2 stitches at each end of the next row. Work

5 rows and increase 2 stitches at each end of the next row (6 stitches). Work 5 rows. Make the toes in the next row: wool forward/around, knit 2 stitches together (through front of stitches), 3 times altogether (6 stitches remain). Work 5 rows. Decrease 1 stitch at each end of the next row. Work 5 rows and decrease another stitch at each end of the next row. Knit 1 row and cast off. Work the other foot in the same way.

To make up:

Sew the head and neck together to about the middle of the neck. The head must be sewn together so it is nice and round. Pin the breast gusset firmly in place and sew it on. Stuff the body with wool before you sew it together completely. Stuff it firmly so it is easier to shape. Sew the last opening together and begin shaping. Bend the head down a little and sew under the chin. Bend the neck backwards a little and sew in the back of the neck. Keep adjusting the tail and back until you are satisfied with the shape. Sew the beak in overlapping buttonhole stitch until it is long and round. Fold the feet in half and sew the edges together. Sew the feet on with buttonhole stitch. It stiffens them so they stand better. You can sew little furrows between the toes to stiffen them even more.

Sew the feet firmly onto the body.
Sew on the eyes with a dark coloured woollen yarn.

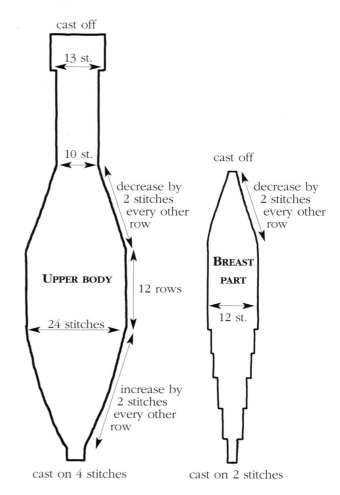

cast off

13 st.

10 st.

decrease by 2 stitches every other row

cast off

decrease by 2 stitches every other row

BREAST PART

UPPER BODY

12 rows

24 stitches

12 st.

increase by 2 stitches every other row

cast on 4 stitches

cast on 2 stitches

Hoppy Legs the hare racing over sticks and stones

Materials

Angora and kid mohair is used here, as for the cuddly bunny on page 42. See the reference regarding yarn on the previous page. See drawings on page 38.

BODY AND HEAD: knitted in one piece. Cast on 20 stitches and work in garter stitch until there are 32 rows. Cast off.

EARS: cast on 5 stitches and work 20 rows. On the next row knit the 2nd and the 3rd stitches together. Knit 1 row and repeat, decreasing twice more. Cast off the last 2 stitches.

TAIL: cast on 8 stitches and work 7 rows. Cast off.

To make up:

Sew the body together so the rows run from side to side. Make a firm little ball of wool and put it in the body. This will be the hare's head. Sew it in at the neck and then fill the body with wool until it is good and firm. Sew the body together at the bottom. Sew the ears firmly onto the head. Make a little woollen ball and place it in the sewn-together part for the tail. Sew the tail onto the hare. You can sew the eyes and nose on discreetly, but it is not always necessary. The hare has its own expression, enhanced by the long ears, and most children will recognise it instantly, with or without a nose and eyes.

Any yarn with an appropriate hare-colour
can be used here. As a rule I use two
different types of yarn, which gives the
best colour structure and surface.
The result is more lively than if you only
use one type of yarn. In addition,
knitting is also a touch faster and
the animal is also easier to shape.

This model is very simple and is
well suited for children to knit.
Maybe young knitters should let
Mummy or Daddy sew and stuff
the hare if they have not
tried it before.

cast off

BODY

32 rows

cast on 20 stitches

knit the 2nd and the 3rd stitch together on every 2nd row

EAR

20 rows

cast on 5 stitches

cast off

TAIL

7 rows

cast on 8 stitches

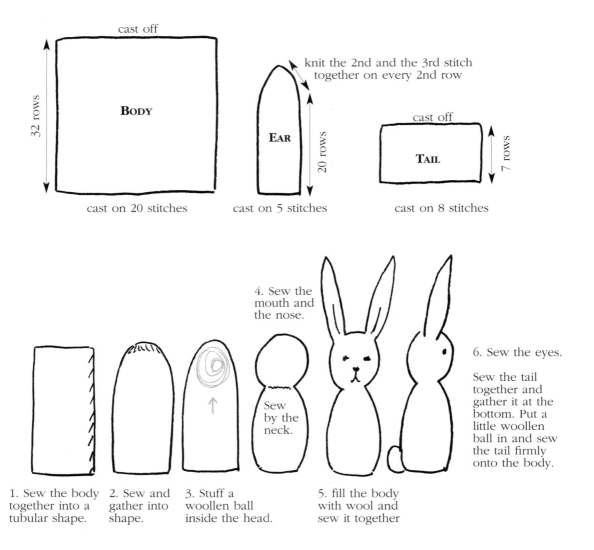

1. Sew the body together into a tubular shape.

2. Sew and gather into shape.

3. Stuff a woollen ball inside the head.

Sew by the neck.

4. Sew the mouth and the nose.

5. fill the body with wool and sew it together

6. Sew the eyes.

Sew the tail together and gather it at the bottom. Put a little woollen ball in and sew the tail firmly onto the body.

Clip, clop, watch the jumping horse

Materials

Here 2 balls of mohair yarn and angora wool are used to make the horse lovely and soft.
Needle size: to suit yarn used
Carded wool for stuffing
Some pearl yarn for the eyes

BODY: cast on 40 stitches and work in garter stitch until there are 12 rows.
Cast off 11 stitches at the beginning and end of the next row, breaking and rejoining the yarn as necessary. Work 14 rows.
Cast on 11 stitches at either end of the next row. Knit 20 stitches, turn the work and cast on 11 stitches in one go. Turn back and continue knitting. This will make a hole which will be sewn together later.
Knit 1 row over the newly cast-on stitches and knit to the end of the row. On alternate rows, pick up 1 stitch before and after the middle stitch.
Work 12 rows and start shaping for the front legs. Cast off 20 stitches at the beginning and end of the next row.

Work 2 rows on the remaining 19 stitches. Cast on 3 stitches at either end of the next row and then 1 stitch at either end of the next 2 rows. Work 6 rows. Decrease 1 stitch at each end of the next row and cast off.
EARS: cast on 5 stitches. Work 6 rows and then keep knitting the 2 middle stitches together until 1 stitch remains. Break the yarn and pull it through the last stitch.

To make up:

Sew the legs together
Sew the head and the 'hole' at the back together. Stuff the head firmly with wool. Roll a woollen 'sausage' firmly around a knitting needle or something similar for the legs.

Place a 'sausage' down into each leg. Make another rolled sausage and stuff the body. Sew the tummy together.
The horse must now have a mane and tail: fix every other stitch firmly, otherwise the mane and tail can be pulled out.
Sew the ears on.

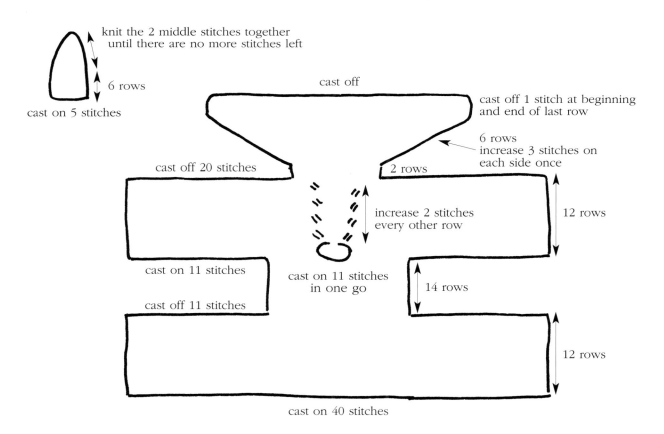

knit the 2 middle stitches together until there are no more stitches left

6 rows

cast on 5 stitches

cast off

cast off 1 stitch at beginning and end of last row

6 rows
increase 3 stitches on each side once

cast off 20 stitches

2 rows

12 rows

increase 2 stitches every other row

cast on 11 stitches

14 rows

cast off 11 stitches

cast on 11 stitches in one go

12 rows

cast on 40 stitches

Clip, clop, see the horses jump
...off they go with manes flying and
flower-strewn harnesses with a carriage
and everything, but who is running
alongside? He looks so tiny...

The bunny is knitted in rather extravagant
angora and kid mohair. But this
gives it the softest look imaginable.
Warning! If you begin knitting this toy, you
must count on being surrounded by children
with a hopeful look in their eyes.
Once you have held such a soft cuddly
bunny against your cheek you won't
be able to live without it…
You've been warned!

decrease

10 rows

cast on 7 stitches

cast off

32 rows

cast on 30 stitches

cast off

11 rows

cast on 22 stitches

Cuddly bunny

Materials

Angora and kid mohair, see above
Needle size: 3mm
Pink silk yarn (or delicat pink stretch
velour) for inner ears

BODY: this is knitted almost exactly like the cat on page 28, and the squirrel on page 32. Cast on 30 stitches. Work 32 rows of stocking stitch. Cast off loosely.

HEAD: cast on 22 stitches and work 11 rows. Cast off.

TAIL: cast on 12 stitches and work 6 rows. Cast off.

EARS: cast on 7 stitches and work 10 rows. Decrease 1 stitch at the beginning of the next 2 rows. Work 2 rows. Repeat decreasing in the next 2 rows. Work 2 rows. Repeat decreasing in the following 2 rows and cast off.

INNER EARS: Cast on 6 stitches and work 12 rows. Decrease 1 stitch at the beginning of the next 2 rows. Work 2 rows. Decrease 1 stitch at the beginning of the next 3 rows. Break the yarn and pull it through the last stitch.

To make up:

BODY: sew the body together in almost the same way as the cat on page 28, but the bunny's back legs must be bigger than its front legs. Sew a little between the legs so they point the right way.

HEAD: fold and sew together at the top and along one side. Gather it together slightly at the top so it is as round as possible. But the pointed part at the side's highest corner must remain slightly pointed. This will be the nose. Stuff wool inside until it feels nice and firm. Gather together at the neck and sew the head firmly to the body. Now it's time to shape the bunny's head before you sew on the eyes and nose.

TAIL: gather the tail at the top and sew it together on the side. Stuff it with wool, gather the lowest part and sew it firmly onto the bunny.

EARS: sew the two ear parts together and place them high on the head. If you place them a little bit backwards and fold them a little, the bunny will have a funny expression.

Chicks, hens & a cockerel

Materials

For the chicks something soft like light yellow yarn (angora is perfect – or alpaca wool, which gives the chick the soft surface you feel if you hold a real chick in your hand).
For the hen, some similar yarn can be used, but also soft woollen yarn or even the hen-coloured cotton yarn. Use the same for the cockerel in a cockerel colour.
Needle size: 3mm
Carded wool for stuffing

Chick

Cast on 10 stitches. Work a little square in garter stitch, about 16 rows. Cast off. Fold the square so it becomes a triangle. Sew it along one side and stuff with wool to form the body and head. Sew the last part of the chick together. Sewing from the flat point up (the back) and back again gives the chick the right curved chick shape. Shape further by sewing a little here and there. Sew with an orange yarn in front for the beak.

Hen

Work the hen in the same way as the chick, just a little bigger, e.g. 24 stitches. You can also sew a little red comb on the head and 'bobbles' under the chin.

Cockerel

Work the cockerel in the same way as the hen, just a bit bigger. Use rich, colourful yarn leftovers for the tail. The cockerel must also have long legs so he can stroll around proudly in the chicken yard and show off. You can use pipecleaners or strong copper wire wound round with the yarn or carded wool in the appropriate colour.

cast off

BODY
(square)

cast on e.g. 10 stitches
(for the chick)

fold

sew together

stuff the wool in through
this little hole

opening

sew from the
bottom upwards
through the
'back' and back
again, pull the
yarn so the back
becomes curved

sew the
beak with
orange
yarn

sew the
eye with
dark yarn

sew the 'comb' onto the
head and under the
beak with a button hole
stitch or knot stitch

make the cockerel's
tail feathers with
colourful nuances

46   *Chicks, hens & a cockerel*

Fergus the Fox

Materials

Fox-coloured yarn (a combination of a terracotta red Shetland wool and an orange-red silk bouclé have been used)
Needle size: to suit yarn used
Carded wool for stuffing
Natural-coloured leftover yarn is used for the tip of the tail
Eyes and nose are sewn in black

Large fox

Body: cast on 30 stitches. Work in garter stitch until you have 10 rows. Cast off 5 stitches at the beginning and end of the next row (these are the back legs), breaking and rejoining the yarn as necessary. Continue working until there are 14 rows (the body).

Cast on 5 stitches again at either end of the next row. Knit 10 rows for the front legs. Cast off 9 stitches at the beginning and end of the next row.

Work 2 rows for the neck.

Begin increasing now for the **Head**: *knit 3 stitches, pick up 1 stitch** repeat from * to ** 3 times, knit 3 stitches (15 stitches). Knit 1 row. On the next row, knit 1 stitch *pick up 1 stitch, knit 2** repeat from * to ** 7 times (22 stitches). Knit 3 rows.

Knit 7 stitches, pick up 1 stitch and knit 8, pick up 1 stitch and knit the last 7.

Knit 1 row.

Knit the first 7 stitches as before, pick up 1 stitch and knit 10, pick up 1 stitch and knit the last 7. Knit the first and last 2 stitches together on the next row.

Knit 2 stitches together, knit 5, knit 2 stitches together, knit 8, knit 2 stitches together, knit 4 and knit the last 2 stitches together.

In the next row, knit the first and last 2 stitches together.

Knit 2 stitches together, knit 2, knit 2 stitches together, knit 6, knit 2 stitches together, knit 2, knit the last 2 stitches together.

Knit 1 row without decreasing.

Knit 2 stitches together, knit 1, knit 2 stitches together, knit 4, knit 2 stitches together, knit 1 and knit the last 2 stitches together.

Knit 1 row without decreasing.

Knit 2 stitches together twice, knit 2, knit 2 stitches together twice. Now there should be 6 stitches left. Knit 1 row.

Knit 1 stitch, knit 2 stitches together twice, knit the last stitch.

Work 9 rows with the remaining 4 stitches. Increase 1 stitch at the beginning and end of the next row (6 stitches). Work 2 rows without shaping. Increase 1 stitch again at the beginning and end of the next row (8 stitches). Knit 1 row. Start decreasing. *Knit 2 stitches together at the beginning and end of the row (6 stitches). Knit 1 row**. Repeat from * to ** twice and cast off.

EARS: knitting both ears separately on one needle, cast on 6 stitches. Work 3 rows in garter stitch. Work the last 2 rows decreasing 1 stitch at the beginning and end of each row. Break the yarn and pull it through the last stitch.

TAIL: take a piece of card 3 cm wide, and wind a little white yarn around it for the tip of the tail, then continue winding using the same yarn as for the body. Sew with chain stitch in the middle to hold the yarn together. Sew the back too. Pull the 'tail' off the card and sew it together in the middle to make it strong and robust. Sew it firmly and cut the loops. Trim it to make it nice.

To make up:

Sew the legs together. Roll the wool into four firm 'sausages' and press them down into the legs. You can roll the wool tightly around a knitting needle or narrow pointed scissors, and press it down into the legs.

Press the knitting needle/scissors with your right hand, while holding the leg with your left hand. This gives a good grip.

Sew the body together towards the neck and stuff it with wool in the same way as the legs. Sew the head almost the same, but leave a little gap open while you are stuffing it. The more tightly the wool is rolled before it goes down into the head, the easier it is to shape it.

Stuff the nose in the same way as the legs. That will make it more pointed.

Sew the ears and tail on firmly.

Now shape it with a needle and thread. Sew the head into shape. It's like modelling with a needle and a thread – pulling the head into shape with the thread which you pull through the wool. Do the same to mark the eyeholes, bridge of the nose etc.

The body also needs a loving hand. It's a good idea to borrow some books from the library with appropriate photos so you know what a real fox looks like.

Fox cub

Cast on 20 stitches and work 5 rows. Cast off 4 stitches at the beginning and end of the next row for the leg, breaking and rejoining the yarn as necessary.

Work 9 rows and cast on 4 stitches at the start of the next 2 rows.

This little rascal
is always on the lookout
for a tasty treat.
The farmer must remember
to lock up the hens
every night after sunset,
or Fergus the Fox, that
sneaky little fellow, may
snatch one of the hens
for his dinner.

Work 5 rows and cast off 7 stitches at the start of the next 2 rows towards the neck. Knit 1 row. Next row: knit 2 stitches, pick up 1 stitch, knit 2, pick up 1 stitch and knit the 2 last stitches.

Knit 1 row. Carry on decreasing until there are 4 stitches left. Work 4 rows and knit two stitches together twice.

Work 4 rows.

Now for the underside of the nose and head: increase 1 stitch on each side (now there are 4 stitches). Knit one row. Repeat increasing at each side (6 stitches). Knit 1 row. Repeat increasing as follows: *Knit 2 stitches at the beginning, pick up 1 stitch, knit to the last 2 stitches and pick up 1 stitch before they are knitted.

Knit 1 row.**

Repeat from * to **, until there are 14 stitches in total. Begin decreasing for the **NOSE**: knit 2 stitches, knit 2 stitches together, knit 6, knit 2 stitches together, knit 2 – knit the next row. Continue increasing until there are 8 stitches left and begin decreasing on each side until there is 1 stitch left. Break the yarn and pull it through the last stitch.

To make up:

The fox cub is made up just like the adult fox. Sew the ears with buttonhole stitch in overlapping rows to make pointed fox ears.

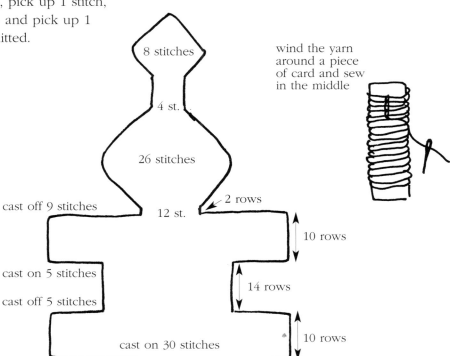

8 stitches

4 st.

26 stitches

wind the yarn around a piece of card and sew in the middle

cast off 9 stitches

12 st.

2 rows

10 rows

cast on 5 stitches

cast off 5 stitches

14 rows

10 rows

cast on 30 stitches

Mother pig with piglets

Materials

The piggies are knitted in leftover woollen yarns dyed with light madder-red (plant dye) and leftover off-white and pig-pink silk tweed, which together give a good pig-like colour. The pigs are knitted exclusively in garter stitch.
3mm needles and 3mm crochet hook
Carded wool for stuffing

Piglets

BODY: cast on 25 stitches and work 6 rows. Cast off 3 stitches at the beginning and end of the next row for the back legs, breaking and rejoining the yarn as necessary.
Work 6 rows for the tummy and cast on 3 stitches again at either end of the next row for the front legs. Work 6 rows and cast off 4 stitches at the beginning and end of the next row for the neck.
Knit 1 row. Next row: knit 6 stitches, *knit 2 stitches together, knit 1, knit 2 stitches together**, knit 6. Knit 1 row. Knit 5 stitches and repeat decreasing as before from * to **. Knit 5 stitches. Knit 1 row. Repeat until there are 4 stitches left on the needle, 6 times altogether. Remember that there are always 2 stitches less for each decreasing row.
EARS: cast on 4 stitches and knit 6 rows. Knit the following rows so that the 2nd and the 3rd stitches are knitted together until 1 stitch remains. Break the yarn and pull it through the last stitch.

Big pig

BODY: cast on 36 stitches and work 12 rows. Cast off 5 stitches at the beginning and end of the next row, breaking and rejoining the yarn as necessary, for the legs.
Work 12 rows for the tummy and cast on 5 stitches again at either end of the next row for the front legs. Work 12 rows and cast off 7 stitches at the beginning and end of the next row for the neck. Work 4 rows.
On the following 6 rows: decrease 1 stitch on each side of the middle (2 stitches on each row altogether).
Knit 1 row without decreasing and then repeat decreasing on the following row. Knit 1 row and repeat decreasing on the next row. Cast off the last 6 stitches.

EARS: cast on 5 stitches and knit 8 rows. Knit the following rows so that the 2nd and 3rd stitches are knitted together until 1 stitch remains. Break the yarn and pull it through the last stitch.

To make up:
Sew the pig's legs together as four 'tubes'. Afterwards sew the tummy, neck and head together. Stuff the pig firmly with wool.

It should be solid and firm and ideally give a bit of resistance when you press it.
Sew the rear part together and sew the ears firmly so that they point forwards. You can sew the eyes on discreetly. The eyes can enhance the pig's expression, but if you overdo it, it can have the opposite effect and look like a caricature of a pig. Be careful and try it out first. Crochet a tail of chain stitches. You can also twist the yarn so the pig's tail curls up nicely.

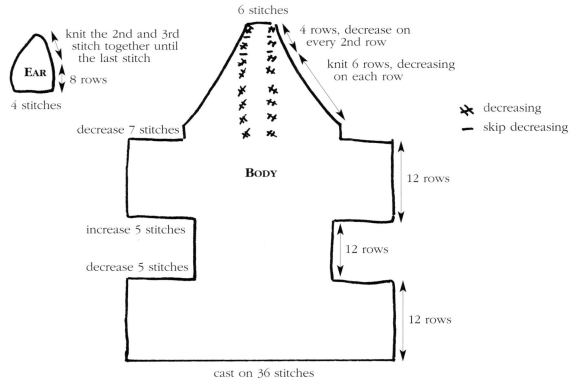

EAR

knit the 2nd and 3rd stitch together until the last stitch

8 rows

4 stitches

6 stitches

4 rows, decrease on every 2nd row

knit 6 rows, decreasing on each row

decrease 7 stitches

BODY

decreasing

skip decreasing

12 rows

increase 5 stitches

decrease 5 stitches

12 rows

12 rows

cast on 36 stitches

Loooong dog...
maybe a dachshund?

Materials

Silk tweed and 2 balls of mohair (decide the colour yourself, maybe find a couple of ideal colours so you can make a look-a-like of the dog you know)
Needle size: 3mm
Carded wool for stuffing

BODY and the head are knitted in one piece. Cast on 36 stitches and work 12 rows in garter stitch. Cast off 7 stitches at the beginning and end of the next row for the back legs. Work 12 rows and cast on 7 stitches at either end of the next row for the front legs. Work 12 rows and cast off 11 stitches at the beginning and end of the next row for the neck. Work 2 rows (14 stitches) for the neck.

HEAD: knit 5 stitches, increase 1 stitch, knit 2, increase 1 stitch, knit 5. Knit 1 row and repeat increasing on the next row: knit 5 stitches, increase 1 stitch, knit 4, increase 1stitch, knit 5. Knit 1 row and repeat the same increasing.

Knit 1 row and cast on 4 stitches for the nose at the beginning of the next 2 rows, while you carry on increasing twice on every other row at the middle of the work. Keep going until you have 8 rows. Cast off.

EARS: cast on 5 stitches and work 2 rows in garter stitch. Increase 1 stitch at the beginning of the next 2 rows (7 stitches). Work 10 rows. Knit the 2nd and the 3rd stitches together on each row until 1 stitch remains. Break the yarn and pull it through the last stitch.

TAIL: cast on 8 stitches. Work 5 rows in garter stitch and decrease once in the middle of the work on the next row. Decrease 1 stitch in the middle of the 12th, 22nd and 30th rows. Cast off.

To make up

Sew the head and the neck together. Sew the legs together as 'tubes' and sew the tummy together. Leave the rear end open for stuffing. You can stuff the legs by stuffing the wool from the paws inwards. Sew the paws together afterwards. It is important that the dog's legs are nice and firm or it will not stand up.

Sew on the ears. Stuff the tail with the wool and sew it on. Sew the eyes and the nose on discreetly. You can also make a 'mouth' for the dog.

Important! If the dog is too wild, you must give him a collar and a lead!

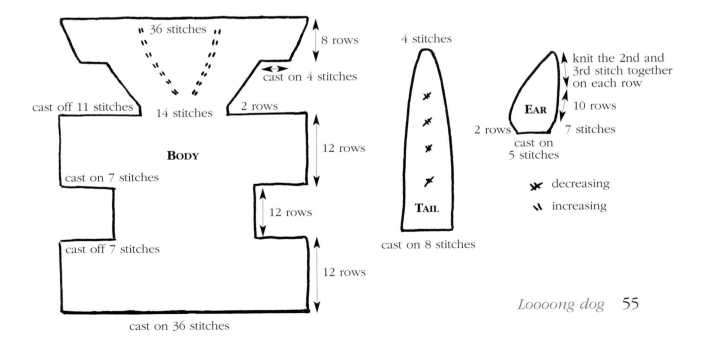

Peter the hedgehog

Materials

Hedgehog-coloured yarn (a combination of a brownish Shetland wool and two different yarns of raw silk in beige and brown colours has been used).
Needle size: to suit yarn used
Carded wool for stuffing
The eyes and nose are sewn on in black yarn, e.g. pearl yarn.

BODY: cast on 10 stitches and work in stocking stitch. Purl 1 row.

Knit 1 row and start increasing towards the hedgehog's bottom; knit 2 stitches, pick up 1 stitch, knit 1 and pick up 1 stitch, knit 4, pick up 1 stitch, knit 1 and pick up 1 stitch, knit the last 2 stitches. Purl 1 row.

Continue with the same type of increasing on the knit rows with the increased number of stitches: knit 3 stitches, *pick up 1 stitch, knit 1, pick up 1 stitch**, knit 6 stitches and repeat increasing again from * to **. Knit the last 3 stitches. Purl 1 row.

Increase on the next row again, giving 22 stitches in total.

Work 9 rows in stocking stitch, finishing with a purl row.

Begin decreasing for the nose: knit 3 stitches, *knit 2 stitches together, knit 1, knit 2 stitches together**, knit 6 and repeat decreasing from * to **.

Knit the last 3 stitches. Purl 1 row.

Decrease on the next 3 knit rows until there are 10 stitches left.

Continue decreasing on the knit row: knit 2 stitches together, knit 1, knit 2 stitches together twice, knit 1, knit 2 stitches together. Purl 1 row.

Next row: knit 2 stitches together 3 times. Purl 1 row. Cast off the last 3 stitches.

To make up:

Sew the body together and stuff it with wool until it is firm and the nose is pointed. Sew the spines on with the two raw silk yarns. Sew with the rya rug stitch (see next page) so that you can cut the loops afterwards. Sew them in tight rows or in a spiral inwards. Sew the eyes and nose with a black yarn. Be creative as you go along as I don't think the stitches have specific names.

RYA RUG STITCH is a kind of backwards and forwards stitch, but in this case, make every other stitch into a loop. Don't actually pull the yarn all the way through. The second stitch which is pulled all the way acts as a 'locking' stitch and ensures that the loops cannot be pulled out when you cut them to make spines.

A poor lost creature, that sometimes visits your garden. You can make a little hedgehog house in the garden and adopt a homeless hedgehog to the great delight of the children.

Peter the hedgehog 57

Pocketmouse

Materials

Leftover grey yarn, preferably soft and nice to touch, e.g. angora.
3mm needles and a 3mm crochet hook
Carded wool for stuffing
Pearl yarn

BODY: cast on 3 stitches. Purl the first row. Increase 3 stitches on the next row, at each end and in the centre.

Purl 1 row and repeat increasing on the knit rows until there are 12 or 15 stitches.

Work 5 rows, finishing with a purl row.

Knit 2 stitches together, knit 1, knit 2 stitches together, knit 1 etc. to the end of the row.

Purl 1 row. On the next row: knit 2 stitches together to the end of the row. Break the yarn and pull it through the last stitch.

To make up:

Sew the mouse together and stuff it with wool until it is firm and hard, otherwise it will easily lose its shape. Crochet a tail of chain stitches.

Sew the ears with 3-4 buttonhole stitches, turn and sew stitches on the top. Continue until the ears are nice and round. Anchor the yarn by sewing into the mouse.

Repeat with the other ear so it is the same as the first.

You can sew the eyes on with some black or grey pearl yarn. If the mouse is white, you can make the eyes red, but that can be a bit scary, so I prefer to make them blue, which is more appealing, as if the sky is reflected in them.

Stealthy little mice
who can hide anywhere
and pop up when
you least expect it.
They are so small,
they can sleep in a
walnut shell.

Glossary

Stitches

GARTER STITCH = knit every row

STOCKING STITCH = 1 row knit, 1 row purl

INCREASE = increase by knitting into the front and back of a stitch

DECREASE = decrease by knitting 2 stitches together through the back of the stitches (unless otherwise stated in the pattern)

PICK UP 1 STITCH = pick up horizontal loop before the next stitch and knit into the back of it

Needle sizes

millimetres	UK no.	US no.
3.0	11	2 to 3
3.5	9 to 10	4
4.0	8	6
4.5	7	7

Ordering books

If you have difficulties ordering Hawthorn Press books from a bookshop, you can order online at **www.hawthornpress.com** or direct from:

United Kingdom

Booksource

50 Cambuslang Road, Cambuslang, Glasgow G32 8NB

Tel: (0845) 370 0063

Fax: (0845) 370 0064

E-mail: orders@booksource.net

USA/North America

SteinerBooks

PO Box 960, Herndon

VA 20172-0960, USA

Tel: (800) 856 8664

Fax: (703) 661 1501

E-mail: service@steinerbooks.org